To Alyssa —
Best wishes,

JAPAN

A TRUE BOOK

by
Ann Heinrichs

Children's Press®

A Division of Grolier Publishing

New York London Hong Kong Sydney
Danbury, Connecticut

Reading Consultant
Linda Cornwell
Learning Resource Consultant
Indiana Department of
Education

A Japanese shrine

Library of Congress Cataloging-in-Publication Data

Heinrichs, Ann.
Japan / Ann Heinrichs.
    p.   cm. — (A true book)
    Includes index.
    Summary: Introduces the history, geography, economy, people, and
culture of the Land of the Rising Sun.
    ISBN 0-516-20336-3 (lib.bdg.)   0-516-26172-X (pbk.)
    1. Japan—Juvenile literature. [1. Japan.] I. Title. II. Series.
DS806.H35   1997
952—dc20
                                                                      96-24971
                                                                         CIP
                                                                          AC

Contents

Land of the Rising Sun

Japan is an island country located east of the mainland of Asia. It is made up of a long, narrow group of islands. The four main islands are Honshu (the largest), Hokkaido, Kyushu, and Shikoku. There are more than three thousand smaller islands. Together, they have about the same land area as the state of California. Across the Sea of Japan to its north and west are Russia and South Korea. To the east, where the sun rises, Japan borders the Pacific Ocean. The Japanese call their nation Nippon, which means "Land of the Rising Sun."

Japan has a spectacular landscape. Mountains and hills cover most of the land. A chain of mountains runs down the

Japan is a diverse and beautiful country.

center of Japan. Snow-capped
Mount Fuji, Japan's highest
peak, towers over Honshu
island. Swift streams flow from
the mountains into the sea.

Mount Fuji (left) is the highest mountain in Japan. The Japanese enjoy the pink blooms of the cherry trees (below).

Dense forests cover the mountainsides where deer and monkeys make their homes. In the spring, the countryside is colored pink and white with the blossoms of plum and cherry trees.

In southern Japan, summers are long and hot. In the north, winters are cold and snowy. Central Japan has a pleasant climate, with warm summers and cool winters. The country is often shaken by volcanic eruptions and earthquakes.

How the Japanese Live

More than 125 million people live in Japan—about one-half the population of the United States. About 99 of every 100 people in Japan are ethnic Japanese. Koreans are the largest minority group.

Japan's largest cities are found on Honshu island.

Most of the people who live in Japan are ethnic Japanese (above). Tokyo is the capital of Japan (left).

Tokyo, Japan's capital, is on the southeast coast. Other large cities are Yokohama, Osaka, Nagoya, and Kyoto. Three-fourths of Japan's people live in cities.

東 京
とうきょう
Tōkyō

The Japanese language is written with characters, or symbols. Each character stands for a word or a syllable. This is different from English, in which several characters, or letters, spell out a word. Japan first adopted the Chinese writing system, then added its own characters.

Buddhism and Shinto are Japan's major religions. Shinto is Japan's oldest religion. Buddhism, imported from China, gained many followers.

A Japanese couple prepares for their wedding ceremony.

Some Japanese observe both religions. Weddings may be Shinto rituals, while funerals might follow Buddhist practices. Temples and shrines of both faiths are found throughout Japan.

City dwellers live in apartments. In the countryside, homes often have tile roofs and walled gardens. Before entering a Japanese house, visitors remove their shoes. The front part of the house is

A Japanese family's living area (above) is usually in one large room. Visitors to Japanese homes leave their shoes outside the door (right).

used for entertaining guests. Floors are covered with straw mats called *tatami*. People sit on large cushions instead of couches and chairs.

The back rooms of the house are the family's living area. Often there is one large room for living, eating, and sleeping. The Japanese sleep on thick cotton mattresses called futons. Dining tables are low, and people usually sit on the floor.

In Japan, people eat with chopsticks. Rice is served at almost every meal, and seafood is often the main course. Sushi is raw seafood

Japanese enjoy meals of rice, seafood, sushi, vegetables, and beef.

dipped in a tangy sauce. Other favorite foods are tempura (batter-fried fish and vegetables) and sukiyaki (strips of beef and vegetables).

Most Japanese wear Western-style clothing—from jeans and T-shirts to high-fashion designer outfits. Some women, however, prefer to wear kimonos. A kimono is a long robe with wide sleeves and a broad sash that is wrapped around the waist. Many Japanese schoolchildren wear uniforms. Children study very hard. Many students take extra classes after school or study with private tutors.

Most Japanese wear Western-style clothing, but some women prefer to wear kimonos (above). Education is very important in Japan. Parents often help their children with their homework (left).

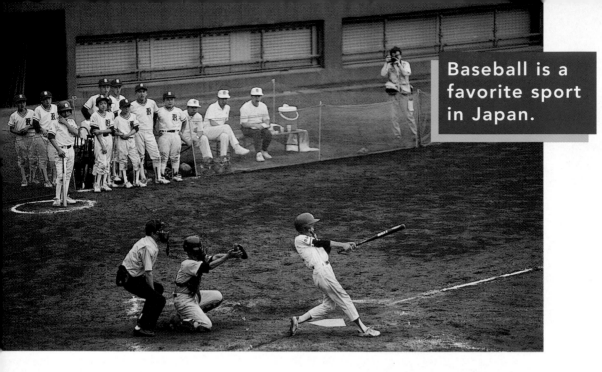

Baseball is a favorite sport in Japan.

Many Japanese enjoy the popular martial arts of judo, karate, and aikido. Sumo wrestling is an ancient sport that is still very popular. Besides their traditional sports, the Japanese love to play baseball and golf.

Bonsai

The word bonsai means "tray-planted." Bonsai is the art of growing miniature trees in a tray or small container. Most bonsai trees range in height from 2 inches (5 centimeters) to 3 feet (91 centimeters). They can be grown indoors or outdoors. It takes a lot of time and patience to grow a bonsai tree. But some bonsai trees can live for hundreds of years!

Emperors, Shoguns, and Samurai

Japan's first powerful rulers were chiefs from the Yamato region. During the Yamatos' rule, many visitors from other lands came to Japan. Scholars from China brought the Chinese writing system in the 400s. They also brought the

Visitors came to Japan to trade and share ideas.

teachings of Confucius. In the 500s, the Chinese introduced the Buddhist religion. The Japanese adopted these and many other Chinese customs.

Around the 700s, Japan became a feudal society. In Japan's feudal society, nobles and warlords lived in great castles and owned large plots of land. Peasant farmers worked the land.

People in the warrior class were called samurai. They lived by a strict code of honor and were very loyal. Warrior chiefs called shoguns led the emperor's army. The shoguns became more powerful than the emperor. From 1192 until 1867, shoguns controlled Japan.

European ships first arrived in Japan in the 1500s. They

Samurai warriors lived by a strict code of conduct and were very loyal to their warlords.

brought traders from Portugal, the Netherlands, England, and Spain.

Shoguns of the Tokugawa family came to power in 1603. They believed that contact with other countries in the world was bad for Japan. The Tokugawas also drove out all foreigners and cut off foreign trade.

Japan remained closed to outsiders for the next two hundred years. Commodore Matthew Perry of the United States Navy sailed to Japan in 1854. He persuaded the shoguns to begin trading with the United States. In 1867, the shoguns were overthrown and the emperor was restored as the ruler of Japan.

Into the Modern World

By the mid-1800s, Japan had been closed to the outside world for a long time. The Japanese had fallen behind the rest of the world in many ways. They quickly began to catch up. Schools and industry were improved, and the army and navy were expanded.

In 1931, Japanese troops took over China's northeast province of Manchuria. Soon Japan controlled land as far away as Indonesia, which is more than 3,000 miles (4,800 kilometers) south of Japan.

World War II began in Europe in 1939. Japan drew the United States into the war on December 7, 1941, when its planes bombed Pearl Harbor, a U.S. military base in Hawaii. The United States

Japan bombed Pearl Harbor on December 7, 1941.

immediately declared war on Japan.

By 1945, U.S. leaders wanted to end the war with Japan. A U.S. airplane dropped an atomic bomb on the city of

Hiroshima was left in ruins after the atomic bomb was dropped.

Hiroshima on August 6, 1945. Another bomb was dropped on the city of Nagasaki three days later. On August 14, 1945, the Japanese surrendered.

Following the war, Japan's economy recovered quickly. By the 1970s, Japan was selling goods all over the world. Other countries looked to Japan for ways to improve their industries. Japan soon became a major world power.

After World War II, Japan's economy became very strong.

Economy and Jobs

Unemployment in Japan is very low. Japan has many factories that produce cars, machinery, and ships. Other Japanese–made products are radios, television sets, cameras, and computers. Japanese goods are famous for their high quality. Many Japanese work

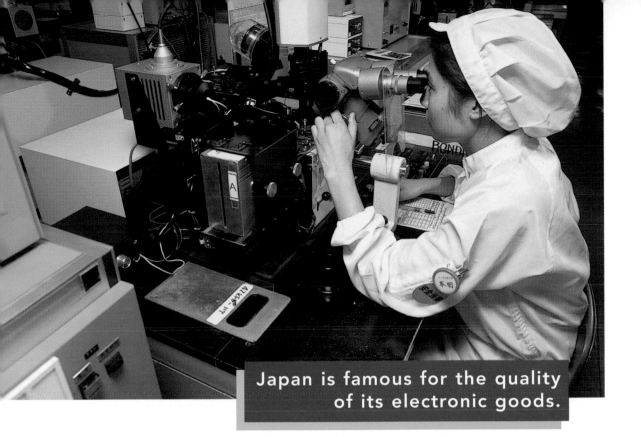

Japan is famous for the quality of its electronic goods.

for large companies, while others own restaurants, shops, and small businesses.

Only a small amount of the land in Japan can be farmed. But Japanese farmers produce

Rice is Japan's most important crop.

most of the food that the country needs. Terraces have been cut into many hillsides for better farming. Rice covers more than half of Japan's farmland. Other important crops include wheat, tea, sugarbeets, and cabbage.

With ocean on all sides, Japan has a booming fishing industry. It sends out more fishing boats and catches more tuna than any other country. Japanese fishermen also catch salmon, pollock, sardines, shrimp, and octopus.

Japan's fishing industry is very successful.

Culture and Arts

Japan enjoys a rich tradition in the arts. One popular Japanese art is called calligraphy—using a brush to paint alphabet characters.

Japanese writers have produced great stories and poems. The *haiku* and the *waka* are Japanese poems.

Calligraphy is an ancient art that requires a lot of practice.

A *haiku* is a short poem with seventeen syllables in three lines. The first line has five syllables, the second line has seven syllables, and the third line has five syllables. The *waka* is a poem that has thirty-one syllables.

In the theater, Japan's No and Kabuki plays tell dramatic stories and use spectacular costumes and colorful makeup. Bunraku is a puppet play using wooden puppets that are about half the size of a person. It takes three people to operate each puppet.

Kabuki plays are very popular in Japan.

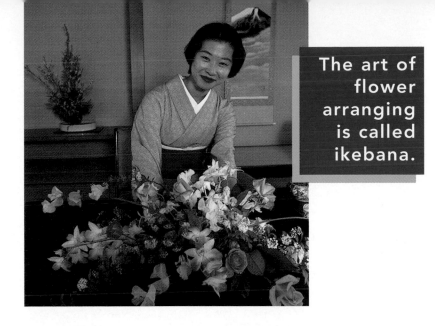

The art of flower arranging is called ikebana.

Many Japanese enjoy bonsai—the art of growing miniature trees. The art of flower arranging is called ikebana. Japan's schoolchildren are skilled in origami, the art of folding paper into shapes of animals or other objects. Birds and fish are popular subjects for origami.

Origami

The word "origami" means "folded paper." Most origami figures can be made without taping or pasting the paper. Here are instructions to make a simple origami figure—a dog.

Cut a 4-inch (10-centimeter) square out of a colorful piece of paper.

Fold the paper in half diagonally.

3. The shape of the paper should look like a triangle.

4. Turn the paper so that the open end is facing you. Fold one of the top corners down.

5. Now your dog has one ear!

6. Fold the other top corner down. Now your dog has two ears!

The traditional Japanese tea ceremony is called *chanoyu.* There are special rules to follow—from how the cups and dishes are placed, to how the server behaves. The *chanoyu* is a very special part of Japanese culture.

The Japanese have great respect for blending with nature. This is reflected both in their arts, and in their everyday lives.

Religion and nature are very important in Japanese society.

To Find Out More

Here are some additional resources to help you learn more about the nation of Japan:

 **Books**

 **Organizations**

Tames, Richard. **Exploration into Japan.** Parsippany, NJ: New Discovery Books, 1995.

Tames, Richard and Sheila. **Japan.** New York: Franklin Watts, 1994.

Tyler, Deborah. **Japan.** New York: Crestwood House, 1993.

Wells, Ruth. **A to Zen: A Book of Japanese Culture.** Saxonville, MA: Picture Book Studio, 1992.

Japan-America Society of Washington
1020 19D Street NW, LL40
Washington, DC 20036

Japan Foundation
152 West 57th Street
New York, NY 10019

National Association of Japan-America Societies
333 East 47th Street
New York, NY 10017

U.S.-Japan Culture Center
2600 Virginia Avenue NW, Suite 711
Washington, DC 20037

Online Sites

Japan, My Japan
*http://lang.nagoya-u.
ac.jp/~matsuoka/Japan.
html*

Facts and figures, current events, information about the government, travel, sports, art galleries, food, and more

Links About Japan
*http://www.iac.co.jp/
~daccordo/jlinks.html*

Visit a Buddhist temple, learn about major events in Japanese history, and take a walking tour of Tokyo.

Professional Baseball
*http://www.inter.co.jp/
Baseball/*

Who's leading the Japanese League in home runs? Find out, along with other current statistics, career records, team schedules, and more.

Try Origami
*http://www.cs.ubc.ca/
spider/jwu/origami.html*

This site is complete with instructions you'll need to get started creating your own origami figures.

Important Words

ethnic relating to a person's racial, national, religious, or cultural background

foreigners people in a country who are from a different country

feudal society social system in which common people work land owned by a lord or noble, and pay him with crops or services

miniature very small

traditions long-held beliefs and customs

Western anything that relates to the culture in Europe or the United States

Index

Meet the Author

Ann Heinrichs grew up in Arkansas and lives in Chicago, Illinois. She has written more than twenty books on American, Asian, and African history and culture.

Ms. Heinrichs has traveled throughout the United States, Europe, North Africa, the Middle East, and east Asia. The desert is her favorite terrain.

Ms. Heinrichs holds bachelor's and master's degrees in piano performance. For relaxation, she practices chi gung and t'ai chi.